Grade 7

Focus on Faith

This book belongs to

_____

My parish is

_____

Annotated

BROWN ROA
Publishing Media

This edition of *Focus on Faith Annotated Activity Book* was developed by Janie Gustafson.

Copyright© 1991 BROWN Publishing—ROA Media
Manufactured in the United States of America

ISBN 0-697-02862-3

10 9 8 7 6 5 4 3 2 1

Contents

Complete the following statements: [Answers will vary.]

I believe...

I think...

I hope...

I know...

	Things I Once Believed [Answers will vary.]	Why I Believed Them
1.		
2.		
3.		
4.		

	I Do Not Believe [Answers will vary.]	Why I Do Not Believe
1.		
2.		
3.		
4.		

	Five Years Ago I Believed	**Now I Believe**
	[Answers will vary.]	
God		
Jesus		
Church		
Prayer		

Re-read Matthew 8:5–13 and Luke 5:17–25. Choose one and then write a modern-day version involving a seventh grader and faith.

[Writings will vary.]

Beliefs of the World

Below are listed the names of religions discussed in your textbooks, some of the beliefs that are associated with them, and a symbol that has come to be associated with each religion. Read the list of beliefs carefully, and match each to its religion.

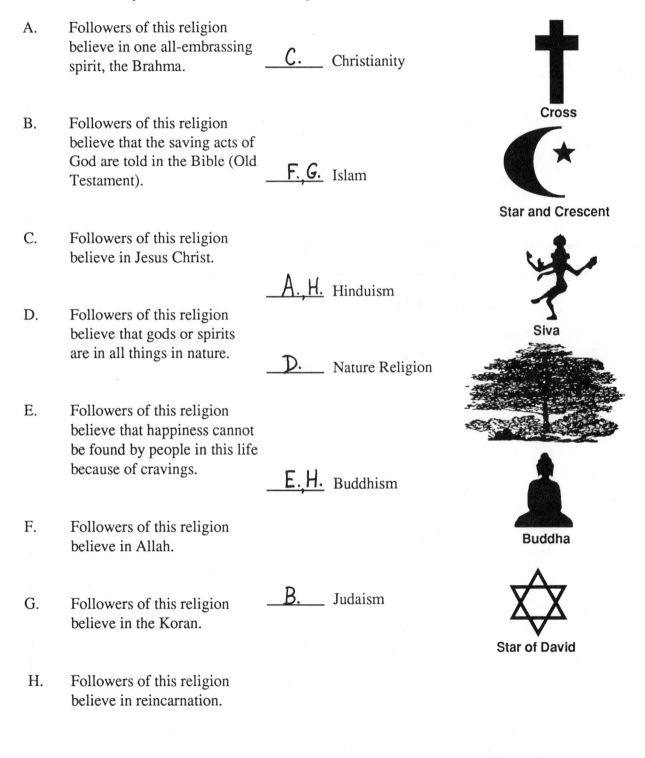

A.   Followers of this religion believe in one all-embrassing spirit, the Brahma.

   _C._ Christianity

B.   Followers of this religion believe that the saving acts of God are told in the Bible (Old Testament).

   _F., G._ Islam

C.   Followers of this religion believe in Jesus Christ.

   _A., H._ Hinduism

D.   Followers of this religion believe that gods or spirits are in all things in nature.

   _D._ Nature Religion

E.   Followers of this religion believe that happiness cannot be found by people in this life because of cravings.

   _E., H._ Buddhism

F.   Followers of this religion believe in Allah.

G.   Followers of this religion believe in the Koran.

   _B._ Judaism

H.   Followers of this religion believe in reincarnation.

Cross

Star and Crescent

Siva

Buddha

Star of David

3

[Responses will vary.]

One Belief I Have. . .

A Symbol of this Belief

World Religions

3	5	6	7	8
God	adore	belief	atheism	Baptists
	Allah	Brahma	Creator	Buddhism
	Bible	Buddha	Judaism	cravings
4	faith	Christ	Moslems	Hinduism
acts	Islam	forces		Mohammed
	Jesus	nature		petition
	Koran	spirit		religion
	power	thanks		response

9	10	11	12	13
believers	discipline	forgiveness	Christianity	reincarnation
Catholics	Methodists			
covenants	Siddhartha			
happiness				
Lutherans				

How Much Do You Know?

Below are 18 statements about Jesus with some possible answers. Circle the letter, or letters, in front of the answers you think are correct.

1. Jesus was born in
(a) Jerusalem
(b) Nazareth
(c) Bethlehem
(d) Galilee
(e) Egypt

2. Jesus lived
(a) about 5,000 years ago
(b) about 2,000 years ago
(c) about 1,000 years ago
(d) just before the Civil War

3. As a boy, Jesus grew up in
(a) Nazareth
(b) Jerusalem
(c) Bethlehem
(d) Rome

4. Jesus lived to about the age of
(a) sixty
(b) forty-five
(c) thirty-three
(d) twenty-five

5. Jesus preached and taught about
(a) ten years
(b) fifteen years
(c) three years
(d) twenty-five years

6. Jesus was
(a) crucified
(b) stabbed
(c) beheaded
(d) shot

7. Christians believe that Jesus was
(a) only human
(b) only divine
(c) human and divine
(d) God pretending to be human

8. Jesus was
(a) a Roman
(b) a Greek
(c) a Jew
(d) an American
(e) an Italian

9. Jesus was
(a) a political leader
(b) a social worker
(c) a Catholic priest
(d) a rabbi
(e) none of the above

10. We know about Jesus from
(a) diaries he kept
(b) the Old Testament
(c) the New Testament
(d) a biography written by St. Peter

11. One of the following was not an Apostle
(a) Matthew
(b) Mark
(c) Peter
(d) Paul
(e) John

12. Jesus probably had
(a) light hair
(b) dark hair
(c) brown hair
(d) red hair
(e) blond hair

6

13. Jesus rose from the dead on
(a) Saturday
(b) Sunday
(c) Monday
(d) right away

14. Jesus lived in Egypt for a time because
(a) Joseph feared Herod might kill him
(b) the Jews and the Arabs had signed a peace treaty
(c) Joseph found work there
(d) Mary thought the climate would be good for Jesus' asthma

15. Nazareth is located in
(a) Europe
(b) North Africa
(c) Israel
(d) South America
(e) Mexico

16. Jesus was born in Bethlehem because
(a) Joseph was looking for work there
(b) Mary's parents lived there and they promised to help her during the birth
(c) Bethlehem had the best hospitals
(d) the Roman emperor had ordered a census and most Jews went to their home town to register.

17. When Jesus became an adult he moved from Nazareth to
(a) Capernaum
(b) Jerusalem
(c) Cana
(d) Rome
(e) Bethlehem

18. On Sundays Jesus went
(a) to Mass
(b) to the Temple
(c) to the beach
(d) to the synagogue
(e) none of the above

[Answers will vary.]

On a scale from 0 - 10, rate how well you <u>know</u> Jesus.

0   1   2   3   4   5   6   7   8   9   10

not at   very

all   well

What are three things regarding Jesus that you would like to know more about?

1. _____

2. _____

3. _____

On a scale from 0 - 10, rate how difficult or how easy it is for you to believe that Jesus is the Son of God.

0   1   2   3   4   5   6   7   8   9   10

very   easy

difficult

Fill in the chart below

	Alternatives to Belief in Jesus	Consequences	Comparison with Belief in Jesus
1.			
2.			
3.			
4.			
5.			

3: Who Is Jesus?
Activity 3

Jesus Word-Gram   [Word-Grams will vary.]

Use the following graph to make a word-gram that contains clues about who Jesus is and how he lived on earth. Try to include all the words below in the word-gram. Then trade pages with a classmate and try to find the words in each other's puzzles.

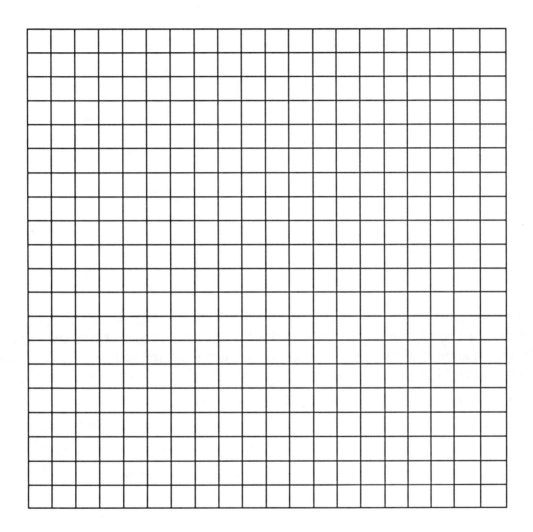

apostles	gospel	Joseph	Pontius Pilate
Bethlehem	human	Mary	Preach
Christ	Israel	Messiah	Resurrection
crucifixion	Jerusalem	miracles	Savior
divine	Jesus	Nazareth	Son of God
Galilee	Jewish	parables	synagogue

The Past and the Future

[Answers will vary.]

In the space provided, tell some things that you know about your great grandparents, or grandparents who have died. How do you know these things about them?

What are some ways in which people who will live a hundred years from now might be able to know you? What stories, pictures, and items will tell your great grandchildren what you are like?

A Modern-Day Evangelist

Read the different New Testament accounts of the multiplication of the loaves (Matthew 14:13-21; Mark 6:32-44; Luke 9:10-17; John 6:1-15). Then write about this event as though you were a newspaper reporter. What message about Jesus does your story give to people?

[Stories will vary.]

EXTRA   EXTRA

Gospel Herald

TODAY'S EDITION • DAILY NEWSPAPER • VOL.1 NO. 1

The Liturgy of the Word

In the missalette, read the Scripture passages for next Sunday's Mass. Give a summary of each passage. Then tell what the passage says about Jesus or his message. Finally, explain how the passage applies to your life.

[Answers will vary.]

First Reading:
> **Summary:**
>
> *Jesus:*
>
> *Me:*

Responsorial Psalm:
> **Summary:**
>
> *Jesus:*
>
> *Me:*

Second Reading:
> **Summary:**
>
> *Jesus:*
>
> *Me:*

Gospel:
> **Summary:**
>
> *Jesus:*
>
> *Me:*

Success and Happiness

No matter what career people choose, they all want the same two things: success and happiness. Look through recent magazines to find out how the world defines "success and happiness." According to the ads, what does a person need in order to be successful, to be happy? Then look through the Gospels to find out how Jesus defines "success and happiness." Finally, write or draw your own magazine ad, "selling" Jesus' formula for success and happiness.

What magazine ads say about success and happiness:	What Jesus says about success and happiness:
that success and happiness depend upon material and external things	that success and happiness depend upon loving and trusting God and loving and caring about others

Your Ad [Ads will vary.]

Building God's Kingdom

Jesus gave us two laws about how to build God's kingdom: love God and love our neighbors as we love ourselves. In the space below, write down ten laws that you think might help to build God's kingdom this year in your religion classroom. After you have written down your suggestions, compare them to the laws suggested by other classmates. Work together as a class to come up with ten laws that everyone agrees on. Write these laws in the right-hand column.

[Answers will vary.]

My Ten Laws	**Our Ten Laws**
1.	1.
2.	2.
3.	3.
4.	4.
5.	5.
6.	6.
7.	7.
8.	8.
9.	9.
10.	10.

What are ten laws that would help to build God's kingdom in your family?

1.	6.
2.	7.
3.	8.
4.	9.
5.	10.

Faith License

You are an official representative of Jesus on earth. To demonstrate your knowledge of the message of Jesus you are to draw up the requirements for being a card-carrying licensed believer in Jesus. Read the list of proposed requirements below and circle the five which you think are <u>most important</u> for a follower of Jesus to have. [Answers will vary.]

A licensed Christian must possess the following:

A. Qualities
1. Loving
2. Patient
3. Kind
4. Able to endure
5. Helpful
6. Understanding
7. Willing to share

B. Characteristics
1. Has faith
2. Wears dark clothes during Lent
3. Believes in Jesus
4. Wants to be a Christian
5. Has passed an initiation test
6. Is not ashamed of being a Christian
7. Is willing to accept Church teaching
8. Has at least one cross in the kitchen, bedroom, dining room

C. Knowledge
1. Has memorized the Ten Commandments, Beatitudes, and other prayers
2. Knows something about the history of Christianity
3. Can adequately answer the following question: Why do you believe in Jesus?
4. Can sufficiently explain reason for being a Christian

D. Habits
1. Receives the sacraments
2. Prays to God
3. Is baptized
4. Goes to confession
5. Goes to church on Sunday

Before licensing can go into effect, you must settle the following issues: [Answers will vary.]
1. How and when will people renew their licenses?

2. Will a teenager need an instruction permit or special training before getting a license?

3. Will there be different types of believers?

4. Will you require a written exam? If so, what would it look like?

5. Will there be penalties for unlicensed believers?

6. What rights will followers have after they pass the exam?

Who Is God?

Take a few moments to think about who God is for you. What image do you have of God? What feelings do you have when you think of God?

In the space below, make a collage from magazine pictures or write an original poem that expresses who God is for you.

[Collages and poems will vary.]

Hell on Earth

Here is a list of things that make "hell on earth" instead of the kingdom of God.

Hatred instead of Love
Fighting instead of Peace
Envy instead of Trust
Jealousy instead of Joy
Poverty instead of Comfort
Hunger instead of Satisfaction
Corruption instead of Honesty
Suspicion instead of Openness
Drunkenness instead of Self-Control
Drugs instead of Clearheadedness
Lying instead of the Truth
Cheating instead of Fairness
Stealing instead of Respect for Property
Sickness and disease instead of Health
Pollution instead of Cleanliness
Divorce instead of Growth in Married Love
Bickering instead of Charity
Abortion instead of Birth
War instead of Peace

From the list, select any four and give an example how each creates "hell on earth."
1.

2. [Answers will vary.]

3.

4.

Now tell how the four things that you selected can be changed to make the kingdom of God a reality.
1.

2. [Answers will vary.]

3.

4.

The God Poll

Read each of the statements and questions below and answer them according to the way you think. At the end of the poll, tally the answers for your entire class and see what others think about God.

Yes	No	
⬤	☐	Everyone has questions about God.
⬤	☐	God wants us to know more about Him.
⬤	☐	Creation teaches us about God.
⬤	☐	God reveals Himself as a saving God.
⬤	☐	God is free from myths and magic.
☐	⬤	The notion people have of God has always been the same.
⬤	☐	God reveals Himself in a human way.
⬤	☐	God continues to reveal Himself to us.
⬤	☐	God put people in charge of bringing His creation into fulfillment.
⬤	☐	God reveals Himself to us gradually.
⬤	☐	God is Trinity: Father, Son, and Spirit.
⬤	☐	God acts in people's lives to bring them to their destiny.

What do I believe about God?

[Answers will vary.]

Clues about God

In each of the puzzle pieces, write one "clue" you have that God exists or a "clue" that tells you who God is. For example, you might write " a beautiful sunset" in one puzzle piece, or "the birth of a baby" in another. When you have finished your puzzle, share it with a classmate. Explain two or three of your "clues."

[Clues will vary.]

Help Wanted

Read through the classified ads in a newspaper, paying special attention to the "Help Wanted" section. Then, in the space below, write your own ad, giving a job description for God.

[Ads will vary.]

V.I.P. Interview

You have been assigned by an internationally-acclaimed magazine to interview God. You must find out how God lives, what God does for fun, and what God's interests are. Summarize your interview in the space below.

[Interviews will vary.]

Good Stewardship

Here are some environmental problems that have appeared in the news recently. For each problem, try to think of ways people could show good stewardship.

Problem	Good Stewardship
1. Some nations produce too much food; the excess rots in storage bins or is plowed under. Two-thirds of the world's people are hungry.	[Possible Answers:] Share the food — systematically and continually.
2. The ozone layer is being destroyed by pollutants. As a result, the earth appears to be heating up, in a "greenhouse" effect.	Establish controls for the elimination of pollutants. Cease production of pollutants.
3. A problem at a nuclear power plant has resulted in detectable amounts of radiation in the surrounding ground water.	Close the plant. Require plant owners to relocate the area residents in a good, safe environment, clean the present area, and close the plant.
4. The rain forests in South America are rapidly being destroyed. Many animals and birds no longer have a place to live.	Make it a felony to cut in the rain forests. Enforce that, and replant on a wide scale.
5. A huge oil spill off the coast of Alaska has killed thousands of birds, fish, and animals, and has polluted the beaches and water.	Require oil company to clean the entire area, pay for all losses, contribute significantly to wildlife restoration, and be inspected often.
6. A large corporation does not properly dispose of toxic substances, such as paint thinner and shellac.	Fine the plant heavily for all violations. Require immediate change, or close the plant.
7. Many highways are strewn with litter.	Raise fines for littering. Patrol for litterers. Suspend drivers' licenses and require six months of road clean-up service.

Destiny Flowchart [Responses will vary.]

Who you will be twenty years from now will depend, in part, on the decisions you make. Each decision "closes" some doors and opens others. For example, the decision to go to a high school that specializes in math may lead you to a career in mathematics. Like-wise, the decision to drop out of school might lead to a low-paying job or to crime.

    Think of two decisions that may face you in the next year or two. Then imagine what the consequences might be for each decision.

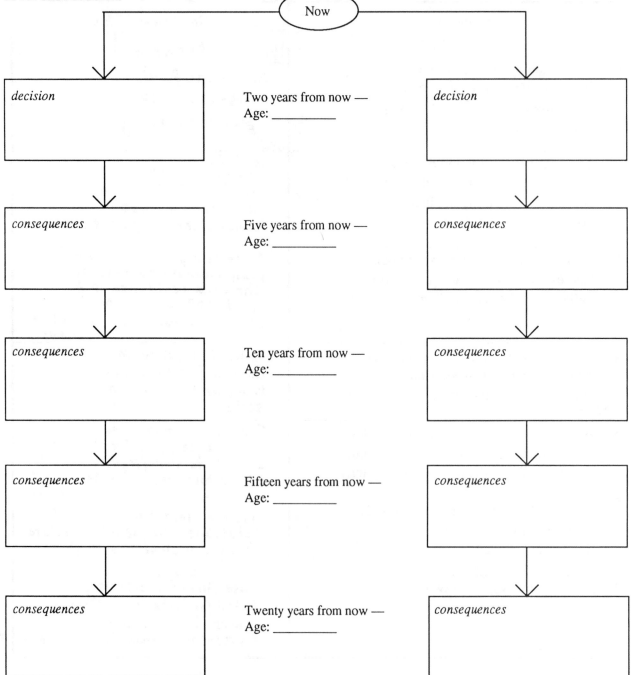

Prayer Thermometer

[Answers will vary.]

1. To see how healthy your prayer life is, think about each of the following questions. On a scale of 0 to 10, measure your present spiritual health. After you have answered all the questions, add up your total score and divide by seven. Then mark your "temperature" on the last thermometer.

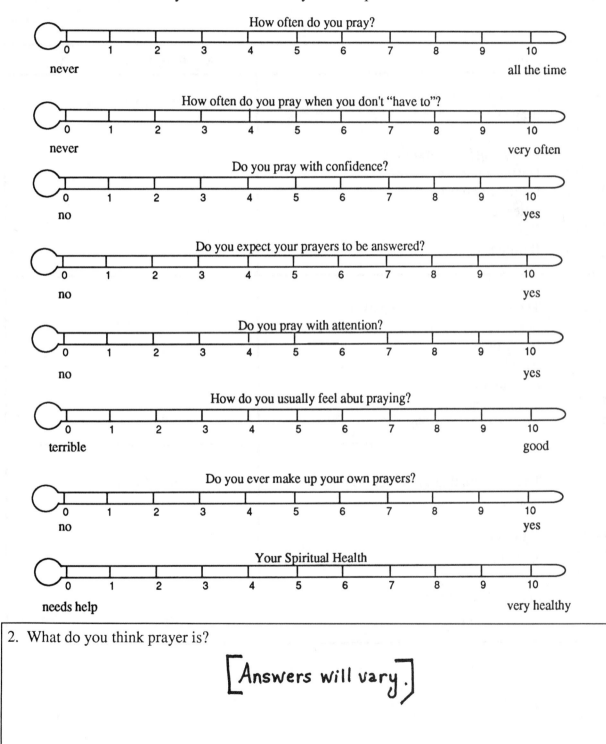

How often do you pray?
0 1 2 3 4 5 6 7 8 9 10
never   all the time

How often do you pray when you don't "have to"?
0 1 2 3 4 5 6 7 8 9 10
never   very often

Do you pray with confidence?
0 1 2 3 4 5 6 7 8 9 10
no   yes

Do you expect your prayers to be answered?
0 1 2 3 4 5 6 7 8 9 10
no   yes

Do you pray with attention?
0 1 2 3 4 5 6 7 8 9 10
no   yes

How do you usually feel abut praying?
0 1 2 3 4 5 6 7 8 9 10
terrible   good

Do you ever make up your own prayers?
0 1 2 3 4 5 6 7 8 9 10
no   yes

Your Spiritual Health
0 1 2 3 4 5 6 7 8 9 10
needs help   very healthy

2. What do you think prayer is?

[Answers will vary.]

A Prayer Plan

[Answers and plans will vary.]

Too often, we neglect our prayer life. To improve your prayer life and establish some habits that may be helpful in praying, set up some guidelines for praying.

The Present Situation	My Plan for this Next Week
Yes No The time of the day I find best to pray are: ☐ ☐ First thing in the morning ☐ ☐ During a break at school ☐ ☐ Before or after lunch ☐ ☐ After school ☐ ☐ Before dinner ☐ ☐ Before bed	When I will pray:
Yes No The places I find best to pray are: ☐ ☐ In my own room ☐ ☐ At school ☐ ☐ At church ☐ ☐ At the dinner table ☐ ☐ A quiet place outside	Where I will pray:
Yes No The postures that I find best to pray in are: ☐ ☐ Standing ☐ ☐ Kneeling ☐ ☐ Sitting ☐ ☐ In a meditation position ☐ ☐ In a relaxed position	How I will pray:

Prayer Expectations

Fill in the chart, then read Psalm 8 and write a meditation on it.

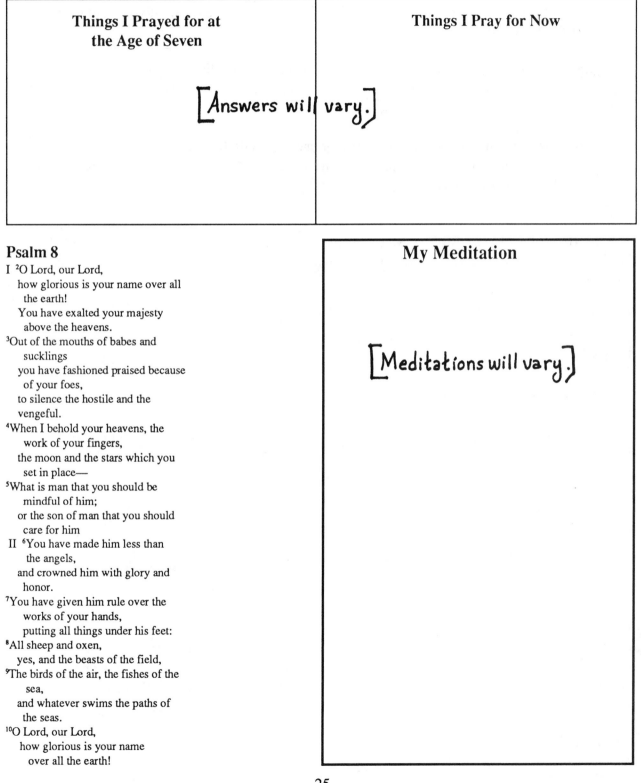

Things I Prayed for at the Age of Seven	Things I Pray for Now
[Answers will vary.]	

Psalm 8

I ²O Lord, our Lord,
    how glorious is your name over all
      the earth!
    You have exalted your majesty
      above the heavens.
³Out of the mouths of babes and
      sucklings
    you have fashioned praised because
      of your foes,
    to silence the hostile and the
      vengeful.
⁴When I behold your heavens, the
      work of your fingers,
    the moon and the stars which you
      set in place—
⁵What is man that you should be
      mindful of him;
    or the son of man that you should
      care for him
II ⁶You have made him less than
      the angels,
    and crowned him with glory and
      honor.
⁷You have given him rule over the
      works of your hands,
    putting all things under his feet:
⁸All sheep and oxen,
    yes, and the beasts of the field,
⁹The birds of the air, the fishes of the
      sea,
    and whatever swims the paths of
      the seas.
¹⁰O Lord, our Lord,
    how glorious is your name
      over all the earth!

My Meditation

[Meditations will vary.]

Prayer Service

Use the outline below for creating your own prayer service. [Prayer Services will vary.]

1. **Choose a theme for your prayer service.** Put down in one sentence what you want to say in your · prayer service.

2. **Choose two readings for your prayer service.** Select your readings to go along with your theme. The readings can come from the Bible or from poetry or any other source that interests
    a.   b.

3. **Decide if you will have music at your prayer service.** Will the music be provided by members of your own class who can sing or play an instrument or will you have recorded music at your service? Select two songs that will go along with your theme.
    a.   b.

4. **Plan the order of your Bible service.** List the readings and the songs in the spaces provided below and write the name of the person who will be responsible for that part of the service.

Opening song or prayer: Reader or Singers:

Statement of the theme: Reader:

First reading: Reader:

Period of silence for reflection

Comments from the group about the   Everyone should add to the service by
Bible reading   making their thoughts known.

Second reading: Reader:

Petitions: The petitions can be silent or spoken.
                                               They can go along with the theme or
                                               they can just be whatever is on your
                                               mind right now.

Homily: Speaker: (Ask your teacher or one of
                                               the students in your class or someone
                                               from your parish or school to speak
                                               on the theme for your service.)

Closing song or prayer: Readers or singers:

Mass Maze

"Why do I attend Mass?" is a question on many young Catholics' minds. The maze below provides some answers. Get to the center of the maze and you'll be free to give the answer that's right for you.

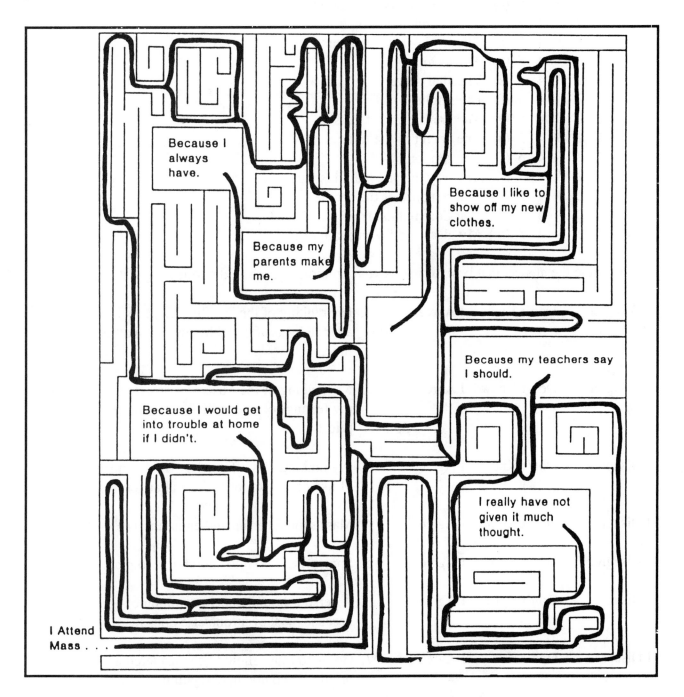

If you made it to the center of the maze successfully, you have avoided some poor reasons for going to Mass. Why do you go to Mass?

Attitudes Toward Mass

[Answers will vary.]

On a scale from 1 to 5 (poor to excellent) rank the following according to the last Sunday Mass you attended:

1 2 3 4 5 (a) The time of day or evening
1 2 3 4 5 (b) The church building
1 2 3 4 5 (c) The seating arrangement
1 2 3 4 5 (d) The lectors
1 2 3 4 5 (e) The altar servers
1 2 3 4 5 (f) The singing
1 2 3 4 5 (g) The preparation of gifts
1 2 3 4 5 (h) The prayer of the faithful
1 2 3 4 5 (i) The sermon
1 2 3 4 5 (j) The way the priest did his part
1 2 3 4 5 (k) The response of the people
1 2 3 4 5 (l) The Communion ritual
1 2 3 4 5 (m) My ideas and feelings after Mass

Now circle the answer that best expresses your opinion on each of the following statements:

I Disagree   Don't Know   I Agree   1. My ranking of the last Sunday Mass I attended was affected by my mood at the time.

I Disagree   Don't Know   I Agree   2. My ranking of the Mass was affected by my feelings of like or dislike toward the priest.

I Disagree   Don't Know   I Agree   3. My ranking was affected by my feelings of like or dislike toward the altar servers.

I Disagree   Don't Know   I Agree   4. Mass should be fun and entertaining.

I Disagree   Don't Know   I Agree   5. Sometimes I go into church just to pray.

I Disagree   Don't Know   I Agree   6. A person should receive communion because most everyone else does it.

I Disagree   Don't Know   I Agree   7. Going to Mass should be considered a privilege and not an obligation.

I Disagree   Don't Know   I Agree   8. We should receive Communion every time we celebrate Mass.

Planning a Mass–Liturgy Preparation Worksheet

Theme _____

       Page____ To read _____ Not to be read _____

       By _____

Opening Song _____ Page____ Led by _____

Liturgy of the Word

First Reading _____

       By _____

Responsorial Psalm

       Page____ To be read_____ To be sung _____

Second Reading _____

       By _____

Alleluia

       Page____ To be read_____ To be sung _____

       By _____

Gospel _____

Homily _____

Creed _____

Prayer of the Faithful

       Priest _____ People _____ Spontaneous _____

       Response _____

Presentation Song _____ By _____

Gifts Presented by *(wine)* _____

                (water) _____

                (bread) _____

                (other) _____

Liturgy of the Eucharist

Holy, Holy   Page____ Sung _____ Not Sung _____
Acclamations

       Page ___ Sung _____ Not Sung _____

Great Amen   Page ___ Sung _____ Not Sung _____

Our Father   Page ___ Sung _____ Not Sung _____

Sign of Peace

Lamb of God   Page ___ Sung _____ Not Sung _____

Communion Song_____ Page ___

Reflection   Quiet ___ Sung _____ Not Sung _____

       Read _____

Closing Song _____ Page ___

Ways to Participate

For each part of the Mass below, describe how you can participate. Then read through the list of liturgical ministries and decide if you might like to serve the Christian community in this way—either now or in the future.

Part of Mass	How I Can Participate **Possible Answers:**
1. Introductory Rite	Respond to the different parts of the Introductory Rite — the Entrance Song, the Greeting, the Penitential Rite, the "Lord, have mercy," and the "Glory to God." Learn and say the responses.
2. Scripture Readings	Listen carefully to the Scripture Readings, following along in the missalette. Respond to the readings, with the congregation. Study the readings at home. Volunteer to be a lector.
3. Creed and Prayer of the Faithful	Learn the Creed and profess it with the people. Study the meaning of the Creed. Know what it is that the Church believes. Listen carefully to the Prayer of the Faithful and respond in prayer, verbally and in your heart, to the petitions.
4. Presentation of Gifts	Think about what is happening. Join in the singing. Volunteer, with your family, to be presenters of the gifts when needed.
5. Sign of Peace	Greet the people around you with sincere caring and with happiness, and wish for them the peace of Jesus.
6. Communion	Think about what is happening. Go quietly and gladly to receive Jesus in Communion. Feel yourself to be one with Jesus, with all people everywhere. Pray to be like Jesus.
7. Dismissal	Join in the singing and in the responses. After the last hymn, genuflect, and leave quietly and joyfully. Most of all, live the Mass... every day.

Liturgical Ministers: altar server, lector, greeter, usher, Eucharistic minister, music minister
I would like to serve as:_____

[Answers will vary.]

Mass Challenge

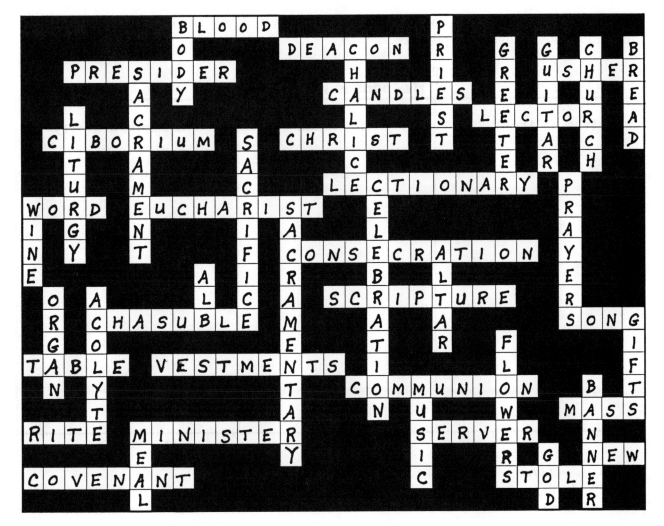

3	4	5	6	7	8	9
alb	body	altar	banner	acolyte	chasuble	communion
God	Mass	blood	Christ	candles	ciborium	Eucharist
new	meal	bread	church	chalice	covenant	sacrament
	rite	gifts	deacon	flowers	minister	sacrifice
	song	music	guitar	greeter	presider	Scripture
	wine	organ	lector	liturgy		vestments
	word	stole	priest	prayers		
		table	server			
		usher				

10	11	12
Lectionary	celebration	consecration
		Sacramentary

Important Things

Decide on one work of art, one invention, and one scientific discovery that has most enriched your life. Write about it in the space provided.

[Responses will vary.]

Work of Art:	Invention:	Scientific Discovery

Make a list—or draw—the signs that you come across in one week.
Then tell why these signs are important.

[Responses will vary.]

Household Blessings

To remind yourself that all times and all places are holy, write a simple blessing for each of the following occasions in your household. When the occasion arises, say the blessing together with your family.

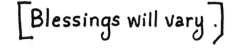

Birthday Blessing:
Blessing of a Wedding Anniversary:
Blessing of a New Family Member:
Blessing of the Christmas Tree:
Blessing during Sickness:
Blessing in Times of Joy and Thanksgiving:
Blessing in Times of Suffering and Need:
Blessing in Times of Penance and Reconciliation:
Blessing before Meals:

Baptism and Confirmation

To investigate some of your own thoughts about Baptism and Confirmation respond to each of the statements below according to the way you think.

For numbers 2 – 6 and number 10, answers will vary.

Yes	No	Not Sure	
☐	⊙	☐	1. Is Baptism necessary for salvation?
☐	☐	☐	2. Would you have preferred that your parents would have waited until you were older and let you decide if you wanted to be baptized in the Catholic Church?
☐	☐	☐	3. When you have children will you allow them to choose the time for their Baptism?
☐	☐	☐	4. Are you glad that your parents presented you for Baptism when you were an infant?
☐	☐	☐	5. Do you ever think about your Baptism?
☐	☐	☐	6. Do you know anyone who is not baptized?
⊙	☐	☐	7. Confirmation is important.
⊙	☐	☐	8. Confirmation is the completion of Baptism.
⊙	☐	☐	9. Confirmation is an act of worship.
☐	☐	☐	10. The gifts of the Spirit are meaningful to me.

Answer the following questions:

How are Baptism and Confirmation alike?

Baptism and Confirmation are both Sacraments of Initiation into the Body of Christ, the Church.

If you have already received the Sacrament of Confirmation, how has it affected your life? (If you will be receiving Confirmation in the future, what do you hope to gain from it?)

Answers will vary.

Rite of Baptism

The Sacrament of Baptism celebrates the beginning of a person's membership in God's family and his or her new life in Christ Jesus. Here is an overview of what happens in the sacrament.

1. Reception of the Child

The priest or deacon greets the child's parents and all present. He addresses the parents and godparents: "You have asked to have your child baptized. In doing so, you are accepting the responsibility of nurturing his (her) faith. It will be your duty to bring him (her) up to keep God's commandments as Christ taught us, by loving God, neighbors, and him (her) self. Do you clearly understand and accept this?" The priest, parents, and godparents then claim the child for Christ and trace the cross on the child's forehead.

2. Celebration of God's Word

One or two of the following Gospel passages are read: John 3:1-5 (Jesus and Nicodemus talk about God's kingdom); Matthew 28:18-20 (Jesus sends the apostles to preach and baptize); Mark 1:9-11 (The Baptism of Jesus); and Mark 10:13-16 (Jesus welcomes the children).

After the homily, the people pray for God to give the child the new life of Baptism. The priest or deacon prays for God to free the child from original sin and send the Holy Spirit to dwell within him or her.

3. Celebration of the Sacrament

The priest or deacon blesses the water for Baptism. The parents and godparents make known their faith by saying the Apostles' Creed. Then, the priest or deacon baptizes the child saying: "I baptize you in the name of the Father (he pours water on the child's head), and the Son (he pours water a second time), and of the Holy Spirit (he pours water a third time)." The child is anointed with chrism as a sign of membership in the Church. "God, the Father of our Lord Jesus Christ, has freed you from sin, given you new birth by water and the Holy Spirit, and welcomed you into His holy People. He now anoints you with the chrism of salvation. As Christ was anointed Priest, Prophet, and King, so may you live always as a member of His Body, sharing everlasting life."

The child is then clothed with a white garment as a sign of new life: "You are a new creation and have been clothed with Christ. See in this white garment the outward sign of your Christian dignity. With your family and friends to help you by word and example, bring that dignity unstained into the everlasting life of heaven."

The child is then given a candle as a sign of Jesus' presence: "Parents and godparents, this light is entrusted to you to be kept burning brightly. This child of yours has been enlightened by Christ. He (she) is to walk always as a child of light. May he (she) keep the flame of faith alive in his (her) heart."

4. Conclusion of the Rite

The people pray the Lord's Prayer and the priest or deacon blesses the parents, godparents, and the child. Everyone answers " Amen."

The Gifts of Initiation   [Answers will vary.]

When you were baptized, you were given seven special gifts to welcome you as a new Christian member of the Church. These gifts are called the "Gifts of the Spirit." Throughout your life, these gifts have helped you to grow spiritually. At Confirmation, the Church celebrates how it has seen these gifts at work in your life.

In the space below, give an example of an action you have done that shows each gift "at work" within you.

Gift of the Spirit	At Work in My Life:
Wisdom	
Knowledge	
Understanding	
Courage	
Reverence	
Right Judgement	
Wonder and Awe	

Think about It

Read each of the statements below carefully. Put an **R** on the line if you think it's all right to do what the statement says. Put a **W** on the line if you think it is wrong.

Answers will vary perhaps, though none of these is "right" to do.

_____   1. Break the windows on a car that seems to be abandoned
_____   2. Copy the answers to a test
_____   3. Talk back to your parents in a nasty way
_____   4. Splash someone with water at the drinking fountain
_____   5. Steal a candy bar at the supermarket
_____   6. Make fun of a retarded classmate
_____   7. Eat a candy bar before paying for it in the store
_____   8. Yell insulting names at a person of a minority group
_____   9. " Borrow " someone's baseball glove
_____ 10. Miss Mass because you don't feel well
_____ 11. Shoplift cosmetics at the store
_____ 12. Speak in a spiteful way about one of your teachers
_____ 13. Get someone involved in taking drugs
_____ 14. Tease someone so much that he or she cries
_____ 15. Cheat while playing cards
_____ 16. Force older people out of the way while walking down street
_____ 17. Be cruel to animals
_____ 18. Spank your little brother if he's naughty
_____ 19. Engage in acts of sex
_____ 20. Drink alcohol
_____ 21. Ignore an unpopular classmate
_____ 22. Lie about someone you don't like
_____ 23. Lie to get out of trouble
_____ 24. Use drugs to get high
_____ 25. Use "four-letter" words
_____ 26. Borrow writing paper from your classmates
_____ 27. Deliberately disobey your parents
_____ 28. Cut initials in a desk
_____ 29. Drink alcohol to excess
_____ 30. Not do your homework
_____ 31. Litter
_____ 32. Cross the street against the light, when no cars are coming

Rules and Reasons

Every group has certain rules that group members are expected to follow. In the space below, make a list of rules that you are expected to follow. Then state why you think each rule exists.

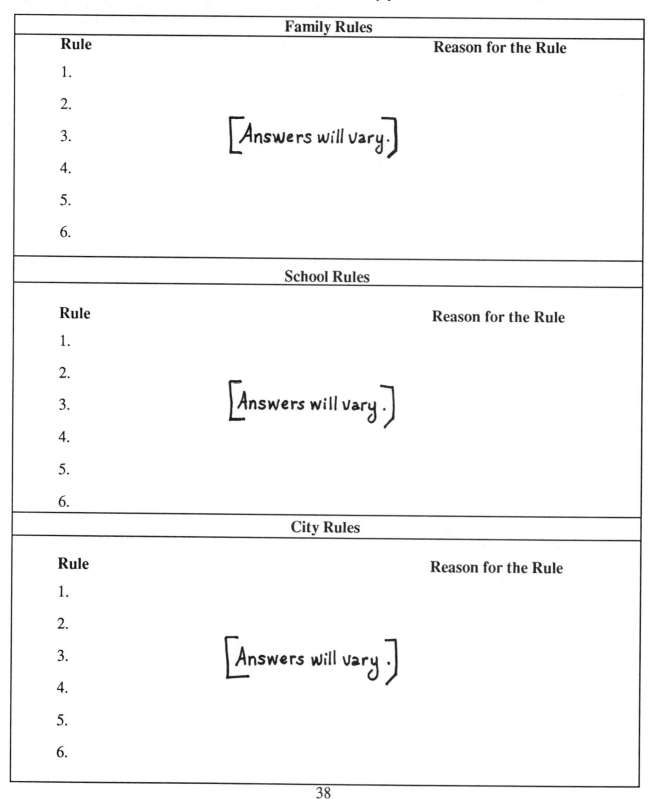

Family Rules

Rule	Reason for the Rule
1.	
2.	
3.	[Answers will vary.]
4.	
5.	
6.	

School Rules

Rule	Reason for the Rule
1.	
2.	
3.	[Answers will vary.]
4.	
5.	
6.	

City Rules

Rule	Reason for the Rule
1.	
2.	
3.	[Answers will vary.]
4.	
5.	
6.	

The Golden Rule

Think about the ways you want others to treat you. Write them down here.

[Answers will vary.]

Now think of ways you can treat each of the following people in the same way as you want to be treated. Be specific.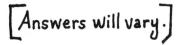

1. A parent	
2. A teacher	
3. Your brother or sister	
4. A classmate	
5. A friend	
6. Someone you don't like	
7. A police officer	
8. The school janitor	
9. An elderly person	
10. A sick person	
11. Someone who is mentally handicapped	
12. Someone who is physically handicapped	

Choices

[Answers will vary.]

Read carefully each of the statements below. Then, using the definitions for *virtue* and *sin* given in your textbook, classify each situation. Put a **V** for "virtuous," an **S** for "sinful," an **NV** for "not virtuous," or an **NS** for "not sinful" before each statement—according to how you judge the situation described. Be prepared to explain and discuss your choices.

_____ Pete cuts the grass because his father tells him to, all the while grumbling about "always having to cut the grass."

_____ Milly accepts a ride home in Randy's car even though her mother told her never to ride with him.

_____ Dave admits he faked illness because he thinks his teacher already knows the truth.

_____ Terry and Mike throw some stones through the windows of an empty house that has a "For Sale" sign on it.

_____ Judy, in a hurry to get to class, stops to help a girl she doesn't know, even though she knows she'll be late if she helps the girl.

_____ Billy and Jason join a group of older teenagers jeering at some black children being bussed to school.

_____ Debbie threatens to tell Jill's mother about Jill's lying in school unless Jill buys her a hamburger and coke after school.

_____ Carolyn makes a remark about her teacher that makes her friends laugh even though she is careful not to let the teacher hear her say it.

_____ Jerry smokes marijuana on the bus going to school and during the lunch hour. He is "spaced out" for about an hour each time.

_____ Mary goes with her friend to help feed bed-ridden patients in a nursing home even though she doesn't particularly like to be around sick people.

_____ Connie hangs around the corner smoking and making nasty remarks about her classmates.

_____ Ed doesn't say anything when his friend steals a pack of pens from the store.

List a cardinal sin and a cardinal virtue. Define each and write about a time you felt that sin and that virtue in your life. *[Answers will vary.]*

A cardinal sin:	A cardinal virtue:
definition:	definition:
A time I felt it in my own life:	A time I felt it in my own life:

Major Life-Situations

[Responses will vary.]

For each of the major life-situations mentioned below, propose a real-life experience a teenager might have. Then list a possible virtuous response and a possible sinful response.

Obedience

Experience:
Virtuous Response:
Sinful Response:

Honesty

Experience:
Virtuous Response:
Sinful Response:

Vandalism

Experience:
Virtuous Response:
Sinful Response:

Language

Experience:
Virtuous Response:
Sinful Response:

Making Fun of Others

Experience:
Virtuous Response:
Sinful Response:

Alcohol

Experience:
Virtuous Response:
Sinful Response:

Drugs

Experience:
Virtuous Response:
Sinful Response:

Sex Experimentation

Experience:
Virtuous Response:
Sinful Response:

Moral Guidelines

The Church bases its moral guidelines on the Ten Commandments. These are listed below. Rewrite the commandments in your own words, as each commandment might apply to your life. Try to be as practical as possible.

[Answers will vary.]

The Ten Commandments	My Moral Guidelines
1. I am the Lord your God... Worship no God but me.	
2. Do not use My name in vain	
3. Observe the Sabbath and keep it holy.	
4. Honor your father and mother.	
5. Do not kill.	
6. Do not commit adultery.	
7. Do not steal.	
8. Do not bear false witness.	
9. Do not desire another person's spouse.	
10. Do not desire another person's property.	

The Rights (and Wrongs) of Employees

Respond to the following statements.

[Responses will vary.]

	Strongly Agree	Agree Somewhat	Disagree Somewhat	Strongly Disagree
1. The most important thing for an employee is to keep his/her job at all costs even if he/she has to do things that are against his/her conscience.				
2. If an employee is paid for forty hours a week, but is able to accomplish the same work in thirty, he/she has an obligation to inform his/her employer that he/she is being paid for ten hours during which he/she does not really work, but just puts in time.				
3. If an employee sees a fellow worker habitually not doing his work, it is his or her responsibility to report this to the supervisor.				
4. There is nothing wrong with taking paper, pens, and other small items from work for use at home.				
5. There is nothing wrong with trying to please the boss in order to get a promotion.				
6. All persons have an obligation to use their talents to the fullest extent.				
7. Employees have a right to strike.				
8. Employees should belong to unions.				
9. There is nothing wrong with taking extra time for lunch or leaving work early if the assigned work is completed.				
10. Employees on one shift should accomplish as much as those on any other shift.				

Answer the following questions:

What do we mean by the statement..."an honest day's work for an honest day's pay" ?

A worker should be paid good wages for good work.
There is a correlation between what one does and the response one receives.

Does the Christian have any obligations to fellow employees concerning the way his/her work is done? Yes. Christians are to be responsible in work as in all areas of life.

Being a Catholic

To investigate some of your own thoughts about being a Catholic, respond to each of the statements below according to the way you think.

[Responses will vary.]

Yes	No	Not Sure	
❏	❏	❏	1. There have been times when I wished that I were not a Catholic.
❏	❏	❏	2. Being a Catholic keeps me from enjoying life.
❏	❏	❏	3. I know that I want to be a Catholic the rest of my life.
❏	❏	❏	4. I would not mind being a Catholic if the Church would change some of its laws.
❏	❏	❏	5. It doesn't matter what church you belong to as long as you believe in God.
❏	❏	❏	6. When I am older I am going to look around for another Church because I don't like having to obey the pope.
❏	❏	❏	7. I can worship God by myself. I don't need a community.
❏	❏	❏	8. A lot of people who never practice their faith claim to be Catholic.
❏	❏	❏	9. In ten years, you will be the same kind of Catholic that you are now.
❏	❏	❏	10. My life would be different if I had been raised in another religion.

[Responses will vary.]

What I Like Most about the Church	What I Do Not Like about the Church

Church History

To help you see how much you already know about the history of the Church, put the following events in the order in which you think they took place.

A. _____9_____ Francis of Assisi, who worked and lived among the poor, dies.

B. _____13_____ Napoleon becomes Emperor of France and gives religious freedom to the French people.

C. _____5_____ Jerome translates the Bible into Latin.

D. _____11_____ King Henry VIII declares himself head of the Church in England.

E. _____16_____ Elizabeth Seton, founder of the Catholic school system in the United States, dies.

F. _____1_____ The apostle James is martyred. Peter teaches in the coastal cities of Palestine. Paul begins his missionary travels.

G. _____3_____ Constantine, head of the Roman Empire, ends the persecutions against Christians and declares Christianity the official religion.

H. _____10_____ Martin Luther complains about Church abuses and breaks away from the Church.

I. _____6_____ The missionary Patrick converts most of Ireland.

J. _____19_____ Pope John XXIII opens the Second Vatican Council.

K. _____2_____ The four Gospels and letters of Paul are read throughout the whole Church.

L. _____14_____ Christianity spreads to Africa, India, and the Far East because of Spanish and Portuguese explorers.

M. _____4_____ The Council of Nicea issues the Nicene Creed.

N. _____20_____ John Paul II is elected pope.

O. _____8_____ The Fourth Lateran Council says that Christians should frequently receive Holy Communion.

P. _____17_____ The First Vatican Council states that the pope cannot be wrong when he teaches a truth of faith or morals.

Q. _____7_____ The Orthodox Church, the Church in eastern Europe, splits away from the Church in western Europe.

R. _____12_____ The Council of Trent begins to reform the Church, in response to Protestant complaints.

S. _____18_____ Father Junipero Serra establishes missions along the California coast.

T. _____15_____ Catholics settle in Maryland.

Following Jesus' Way [Answers will vary.]

To see how far along you are in following Jesus' way, ask yourself the questions below. Make out your own code for answering, then give yourself a "mark." It may reveal some things you are not aware of. (Suggestion: 1 = I care a lot; 2 = I care; 3 = I care a little; 4 = I don't care.)

_____ What is your general attitude toward other people? How do you treat them—not your friends only, but all people? Do you make fun of people less gifted than you are?

_____ How do you control your temper?Are you angry often? Do you yell at people? Is your first impulse to fight, to strike back, to make hurtful remarks?

_____ How do you treat your parents? Your brothers and sisters? Your teachers? Those less fortunate than you are? The sick, or crippled companions? Are you generally friendly?

_____ Do you respect others' property? Do you think it's fun to destroy things—not your own, of course, but someone else's? Do you respect public property?

_____ What do you think about yourself? Do you accept yourself as yourself with your abilities and limits? Do you respect others' abilities and limits?

_____ Do you think about your reputation? Do you sometimes do things that make people think less of you? Are you concerned about making yourself the best person you can be?

_____ Do you respect other persons' reputations? Do you ever make some persons think less of someone because of what you have said about them?

_____ Do you consciously try to make other people happy? How do you feel when other people are friendly toward you?

_____ How do you treat people who belong to minorities?

_____ What do you think about people who "look like foreigners?"

_____ What is your language like? Does it always reflect a sense of your personal dignity?

_____ Do you ever lead others into wrong doing? Into serious wrongdoing?

_____ Why do you go to church? To please your parents? To stay out of trouble? To go through the motions? To worship God? To join the faith community in celebration of and commitment to God's work of saving the world?

_____ Do you ever pray "all by yourself"? Or do you just say the words as you always have without thinking about what prayer is?

[Answers will vary.]

_____ What do you think about God? Is God someone who controls the world like a far-off giant? Does God, the Creator of the entire universe, have a relationship with you that is closer than your relationship with your best friend? Do you turn to God for help and inspiration? Does God really have an influence in your life?

_____ Is Jesus someone who lived far away and long ago? Is he someone whose life still goes on because of your relationship to God and to God's work? Do you think that nobody "sees" Jesus in the world unless they "see" him in you? Do you really think that Jesus is the most important person who ever lived?

_____ Do you think of yourself as the *Church*? Do you think of yourself as *the Body of Christ*? Does your life now reflect Christ's *way*?

Facts about the Church

Answer the following questions. Where necessary, consult a dictionary, an encyclopedia, or your parents for the answers.

1. What is the name of the present pope?
   John Paul II

2. By whom was he elected?
   the College of Cardinals

3. Why was his election special?
   He is the first Polish pope and the first non-Italian pope in 450 years.

4. What is the name of the place where the pope lives? Where is it located?
   The Vatican, Rome, Italy

5. Do you know who designed the church there?
   Michaelangelo, Giovanni de Dolci, and Bernini

6. When was it built?
   in the 14th century

7. How many popes have there been since St. Peter?
   263 since Peter. Counting Peter, John Paul II is the 264th pope.

8. Of what city is the pope the bishop?
   Rome, Italy

9. What is the name of the bishop of your diocese?
   [Answers will vary]

10. What is a diocese?
    a large area governed by a bishop and made up of many parishes

11. What is a parish?
    a smaller area, served by one parish church

12. What is a pastor?
    the head of a parish

13. Who is the pastor of your church?
    [Answers will vary]

14. How many Catholics are there in your parish?
    [Answers will vary]

15. Have you ever belonged to a different Catholic parish? If so, where?
    [Answers will vary]

16. Where were you baptized?
    [Answers will vary]

Symbols for the Church

Some people picture the Church as a stairway, with lay people on the bottom and the pope at the top. Other people picture the Church as a circle. Study the two diagrams here. Then decide which one best illustrates your understanding of Church.

[Answers will vary.]

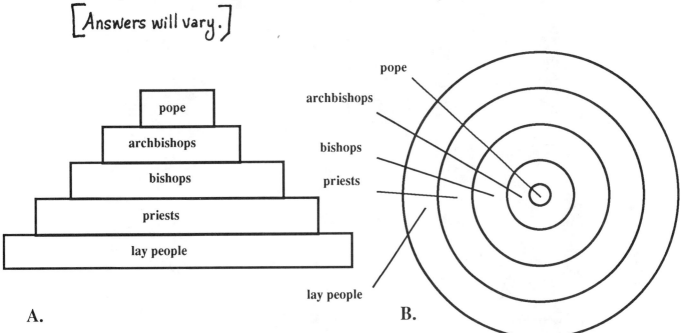

A.

B.

My understanding of Church is like diagram_____

because ——————————————————————————————————

My Symbol

In this space, draw your own symbol of what you think the Church is.

[Symbols will vary.]

Church Crossword

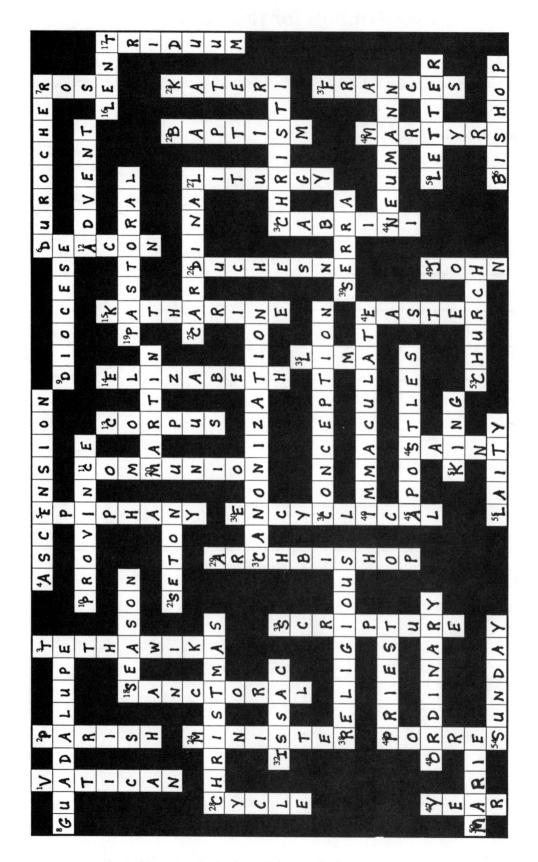

Puzzle Clues

1. The pope, the (_56 across_) of Rome, lives at the (_1 down_). An (_30 down_) is a circular letter written by the pope to all Catholics.

2. A (_25 across_) is a bishop who assists the pope; an (_29 down_) heads a (_10 across_); a bishop heads a (_9 across_); a (_43 across_) leads a (_2 down_), sometimes with the help of (_38 across_) brothers and sisters and a (_6 down_). The members of the parish (_53 across_) are called the (_55 across_). Today, many lay people (_24 down_) to others in the Church.

3. A (_19 across_) (_50 across_) is one way bishops communicate with the people in their diocese.

4. The Church (_47 down_) has five main seasons: (_12 across_), (_28 across_), (_16 across_), the (_41 down_) (_18 across_) and (_48 across_) Time. The three holiest days of the year are called the Easter (_17 down_). Each (_54 across_) is known as "the Lord's day." At Mass, Holy (_33 down_) is read during the (_27 down_) of the Word.

5. Feasts of Our Lord that occur throughout the Church year are:

   • (_5 down_), the first Sunday after January 1;
   • the (_22 down_) of the Lord, the first Sunday after Epiphany;
   • (_4 across_) Thursday, the fortieth day after Easter;
   • (_13 down_) (_34 across_), the feast honoring the Body of Christ; and
   • Christ the (_51 across_), the Sunday before Advent.

6. (_31 across_) is the process by which the Church declares a person a (_46 down_). American saints and heroes include the following:

   • the Mohawk Indian (_23 down_) (_3 down_);
   • the Dominican lay brother (_20 across_) de (_43 down_);
   • Rose of (_35 down_);
   • the Italian nun (_37 down_) (_34 down_);
   • Junipero (_39 across_);
   • bishop of Philadelphia (_49 down_) (_44 across_);
   • founder of Catholic schools (_14 down_) (_21 across_);
   • Jesuit martyr (_32 across_) Jogues;
   • founder of the Sister of the Holy Name, (_52 across_) (_6 across_);
   • heiress (_15 down_) Drexel; and
   • (_7 down_) (_26 down_), who worked with the poor in New Orleans.

   The saints are honored in the (_18 down_) (_28 down_) of the Church year. The (_45 across_) and (_42 down_), as well as other members of the (_11 down_) of saints, are honored in this cycle. Mary is also honored as the (_40 across_) (_36 across_) and Our Lady of (_8 across_).

Important Christian Feasts

To help you grow in awareness of the Church year and the important Christian feasts, consult a liturgical calendar for the next year. Find each feast and write down its date. Also write down the liturgical color of the day.

Feast	Date	Color
All Saints	November 1	white
The Annunciation	March 25	white
Ascension Thursday	40 days after Easter	white
Ash Wednesday	40 days before Easter	purple
The Assumption of Mary	August 15	white
Baptism of the Lord	Sunday after January 6	white
Birth of Jesus	December 25	white
Birth of John the Baptist	June 24	white
Birth of Mary	September 8	white
Christ the King	1st Sunday before Advent	white
Corpus Christi	Sunday after Trinity Sun.	white
Easter	1st Sunday after 1st full moon after March 20	white
Epiphany	Sunday after January 1	white
Good Friday	Friday before Easter	red
Holy Family	Sunday after Christmas	white
Holy Thursday	Thursday before Easter	white
Immaculate Conception	December 8	white
Palm Sunday	Sunday before Easter	red
Pentecost	50 days (7th Sun.) after Easter	red
Presentation of the Lord	February 2	white
St. Joseph	March 19	white
St. Patrick	March 17	white
Sts. Peter and Paul	June 29	red
St. Stephen, martyr	December 26	red
Solemnity of Mary, Mother of God	January 1	white
Transfiguration	August 6	white
Trinity Sunday	Sunday after Pentecost	white
Your Patron Saint	[Answers will vary.]	[Answers will vary.]

Questions about Death

[Answers will vary.]

What are some questions you have about death?

1.
2.
3.
4.

What do you think happens to a person after death? Why do you think this?

What are your present feelings about death?

How do you feel when you think about your own death? Do you believe in ghosts?

Have you ever seen a ghost? Has anyone you know ever seen a ghost?

Does your family or cultural group have particular funeral or burial customs? What are they?

St. Joseph is known as the patron of a happy death because Mary and Jesus were at his side when he died. Write a prayer to St. Joseph, asking him to give you a happy death when you die, or asking him to grant a happy death to someone you love when he or she dies.

Death According to the Gospels

[Possible Answers:]

Read Mark 14:43–15:47. In your own words, summarize the death experience of Jesus.

> The death experience of Jesus was the human experience of death, made most difficult because he was betrayed, mocked, beaten, abandoned, forced to carry the cross and, finally, crucified. Even so, during it all, he forgave everyone.

Read John 20. What was the reaction of the apostles to Jesus' appearing to them? Why did they feel this way? How would you have felt?

> The apostles rejoiced — because they loved him, and because he had risen as he promised. That meant he was truly the Messiah, and it meant that they, too, would have eternal life.

Read Mark 16:19. In your own words, tell how this Scripture passage relates to the Christian belief in life after death.

> This passage relates to the Christian belief in life after death because the risen Christ stayed risen, stayed alive. He ascended into heaven; he did not rise and die again. Rather, he continued living...after death and resurrection.

Read Luke 20:27-40. What does Jesus say about God? What does that tell you about life after death?

> Jesus said that God is God of the living, not of the dead. This means that we, as children of God, will live always.

21: The Mystery of Death
Activity 3

Design a sympathy card for someone who has recently lost a loved one. Perhaps illustrate one of the Scripture passages found in your text. [Cards will vary.]

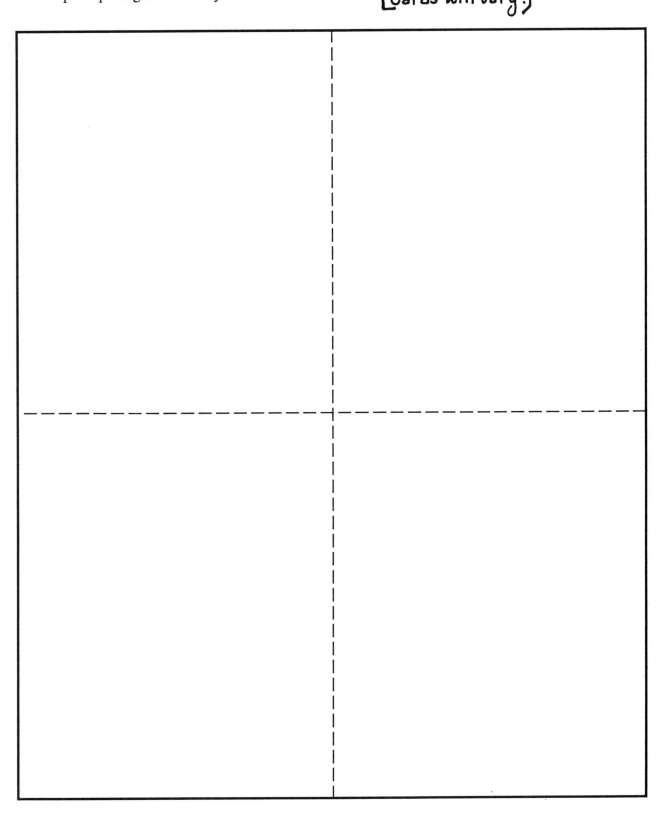

[Cards will vary.]

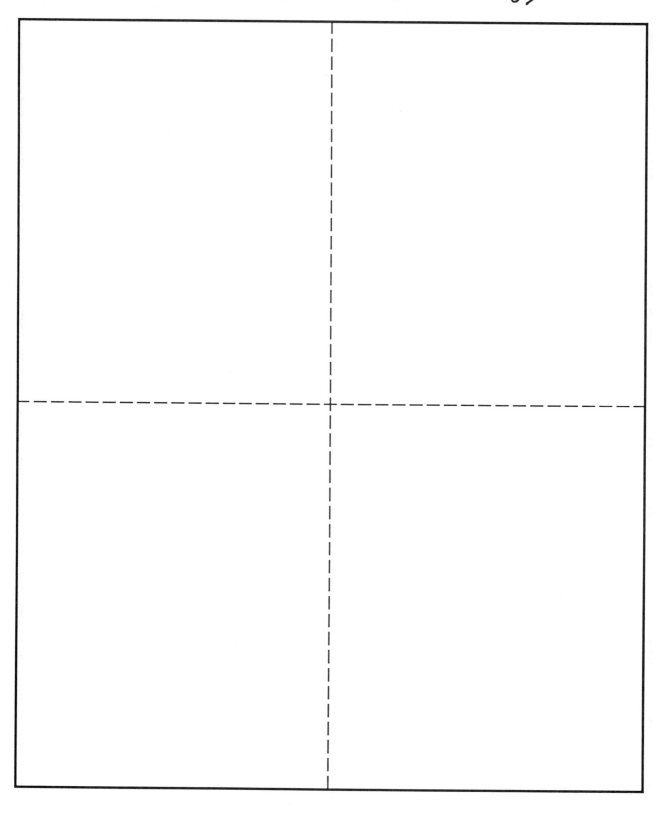

Opinion Survey
[Answers will vary.]

State your opinion on each of the following questions by checking the appropriate box.

Yes	No	Not Sure	
❏	❏	❏	a. Do you think a lot of people would like to avoid death and just keep living on earth forever?
❏	❏	❏	b. Is the kind of "dying" you see on TV the way it really happens?
❏	❏	❏	c. Do you feel the same visiting a cemetery as you do visiting a museum?
❏	❏	❏	d. Do most people you know feel strange when they talk about death?
❏	❏	❏	e. If people really believed they would live forever, would it make any difference in the way they lived?
❏	❏	❏	f. Do funerals give you the "creeps"?
❏	❏	❏	g. Do you think death makes life look very fragile(HANDLE WITH CARE!)?
❏	❏	❏	h. Does the death of Jesus make you stop and think about your life?
❏	❏	❏	i. If you had a disease that was going to kill you, would you want your body frozen until a cure was found?
❏	❏	❏	j. Do people get closest to God when someone they know may die soon?
❏	❏	❏	k. Do you think it would be hard to believe that death ends everything?
❏	❏	❏	l. Do people get "scared to death" when they think about their own death?
❏	❏	❏	m. Do you think people who die live on in memories and dreams?
❏	❏	❏	n. Would it be a lot easier on people if they knew exactly when they would die?
❏	❏	❏	o. Would death be a terrible tragedy if we had nothing to look forward to?
❏	❏	❏	p. Is there anything wrong with killing in self-defense?
❏	❏	❏	q. Is abortion wrong?
❏	❏	❏	r. Do you believe in the death penalty?
❏	❏	❏	s. Is suicide ever justified?
❏	❏	❏	t. Is there anything wrong with driving at excessive speeds?
❏	❏	❏	u. Is it wrong to fight in a war?
❏	❏	❏	v. Is it wrong to kill an animal?
❏	❏	❏	w. Is overeating wrong?
❏	❏	❏	x. Is it ever justified to do anything that harms the body?

22: Eternal Life
Activity 2

Life to the Full [Summaries/pictures will vary.]

Search through recent newspapers and magazines to find stories or pictures of Christians who are living life to the full. Summarize the stories or include the pictures in the appropriate spaces on the next two pages.

People who are helping others grow in self-confidence

People who are helping others believe in God's love

[Summaries/pictures will vary.]

People who are helping others live in peace

People who are working for justice

The Bible Teaches Us

The Bible teaches us many things about the meaning of life. Listed below are possible readings from the Mass for the Dead. Read each passage. Then explain, in your own words, what the passage tells you about the meaning of life.

Isaiah 25:6–9

Lamentations 3:17–26

Romans 5:17–21

Romans 6:3–9

[Responses will vary.]

Romans 8:31–35, 37–39

2 Corinthians 5:1, 6–10

Matthew 5:1–12

Matthew 25:31–46

John 14:1–6

What Kind of Person Do You Want to Be?
[Answers will vary.]

To find out what kind of person you'd like to be, answer the following questions.

1. Describe the kind of person you'd like to be when you are thirty years old.

2. If you could choose the kind of person you'd most want to be like, who would it be? Tell why you selected that person.

3. Describe your best friend by telling what it is you most like about him or her.

4. Describe the kind of person you don't like. First, describe a person your own age, then describe an adult. In each case, tell why you don't like that kind of person.

5. Look back at your description of the kind of person you'd like to be when you are thirty years old. List the things you included in the order of their importance to you. Tell why the first was the most important.

What Kind of Life Do You Want to Live?
[Answers will vary.]

1. Not everything is physically possible. Can you, for example, be a seven-foot basketball player? If you are female, can you be a member of a men's chorus?

   Within your physical possibilities, what would you like to be?

2. Not everything appeals to you. Maybe you don't want to be a doctor or a lawyer, a nurse or a movie star.

   At this moment in your life, what would you most like to be?

3. Not everything is financially possible to you. Perhaps you don't have the money to buy your own airplane or to take a trip to the interior of South America. Maybe you don't have the money now to study to be an airline pilot.

   As you see it now, what would you like to prepare to be, considering your parents' financial situation?

   Does this mean that you will never be able to be what you'd like to be because money is not available to you? Why? Why not?

4. Not everything is available to you at the present. If you don't live near the ocean or a large lake, how can you be a scuba diver? If you live in the city, how can you raise horses on a ranch?

   What should a person do who has an ambition, or a life he or she would like to live, which not now available to him or her?

5. Think about the great number of people who do not live lives they had hoped for or dreamed about.

   Can you think of reasons why they did not attain their dreams or even something nearly approaching their dreams?

A Good Foundation
[Answers will vary.]

The choices you have made in the past have, in a very real way, determined the kind of person you are now. The same is true for the future. The choices you make from now on will determine the type of person you become. Read each of the questions below and start thinking about the type of person you will become.

1. Have you ever read a book which had a profound effect on your life?

2. Do you plan to get married?

3. Do you plan to go to college?

4. Have you ever written a love letter?

5. Have you ever been in serious trouble?

6. Have you ever been seriously ill?

7. Do you believe in life after death?

8. Are you satisfied with the way you look?

9. Are you satisfied with your personality?

10. Do you ever do things just because others expect you to?

11. Do you do things spontaneously or do you think things through?

12. Should you always do what you like to do?

13. Is money more important to you than friendship?

14. If you haven't tried marijuana, would you choose to do so if it's offered?

15. Would you like to raise children differently from the way you were brought up?

16. Do you feel satisfied with your life right now?

17. Are there any adults you admire?

18. Do you consider yourself a Christian?

19. Do you do things because the group does them or because you want to?

20. Are you happy about your faith in Jesus?

Friendship
[Answers will vary.]

In the space below, write your own definition of *friendship*.

What is the difference between a true friend and a friend "in name only"? Do you think it's always possible to tell whether or not a friend is true? Why or why not?

Do you think it's possible to have many good friends? Or can a person have only one or two good friends?

Is it possible to be friends with someone you don't do things with? Why or why not?

What are some of the things you do for and with your friends?

What are some of the things your friends do for and with you?

How Jesus Was a Friend

Read each of the following Scripture passages. Then summarize, in your own words, how Jesus acted as a friend to others.

Matthew 8:1–4

He healed the leper.

Matthew 8:5–13

He healed the centurion's servant.

Matthew 8:14–15

He healed Peter's mother-in-law.

Matthew 9:18–26

He healed the woman with the hemorrhage and he healed the girl.

Matthew 12:46–50

He included all people in his family.

Luke 9:10–17

He fed all the hungry people.

Luke 10:38–42

He reassured his anxious hostess.

John 2:1–11

He turned the water into extra wine for the wedding guests.

John 8:1–11

He protected the accused woman.

John 11:1–44

He brought Lazarus back to life.

What are some ways that Jesus has been a friend to you?

[Answers will vary.]

Stewardship
[Answers will vary.]

To assess what kind of good steward you are now, respond to each question below.

Question	Usually	Often	Hardly Ever	Never
a. Do I respect others?				
b. Am I friendly?				
c. Do I turn people off?				
d. Am I happy?				
e. Am I sad?				
f. Am I easily hurt?				
g. Do I lie?				
h. Do I treat my parents courteously?				
i. Do I smart off?				
j. Do I talk about others' faults?				
k. Do I use drugs?				
l. Do I steal?				
m. Am I selfish?				
n. Do I hurt others by my words?				
o. Do I offer my help?				
p. Am I afraid of others' laughter?				
q. Do I pray?				
r. Can I be trusted?				
s. Do I use vulgar language?				
t. Do I like my brothers and sisters?				
u. Do I hold grudges?				
v. Do I get mad if I lose?				
w. Do I fool around with sex?				
x. Do I use alcohol?				

Look carefully at your answers. Do you like what you see? Do the good qualities outweigh the bad? Would you want yourself as a friend? Answer these questions here.

[Answers will vary.]

Thanksgiving
[Answers will vary.]
Some of the good things that have happened this year:

_____

_____

_____

_____

_____

Five things I have learned this year:

1. _____

2. _____

3. _____

4. _____

5. _____

A time when I have been especially grateful to someone in this group.

_____

_____

A Prayer of Thanksgiving

[Answers will vary.]

Patron Saints of Countries

Most countries throughout the world have a special devotion to one saint. This saint is known as the country's patron saint. To help you discover the patron saints of different countries, match the saints in column B with the appropriate country in column A. Some answers might surprise you! (Resource: *Catholic Almanac*. Foy, Felician A., editor. Huntington, IN: Our Sunday Visitor, Inc.)

<table>
<tr><td>A</td><td>B</td></tr>
<tr><td>1. __H.__ Australia</td><td>A. Andrew</td></tr>
<tr><td>2. __H.__ Borneo</td><td>B. Anthony</td></tr>
<tr><td>3. __C.,M.__ Canada</td><td>C. Anne</td></tr>
<tr><td>4. __K.__ Chile</td><td>D. Boniface</td></tr>
<tr><td>5. __M.__ China</td><td>E. Casimir</td></tr>
<tr><td>6. __W.__ Colombia</td><td>F. Catherine of Siena</td></tr>
<tr><td>7. __T.__ El Salvador</td><td>G. Francis of Assisi</td></tr>
<tr><td>8. __I.__ England</td><td>H. Francis Xavier</td></tr>
<tr><td>9. __L.__ France</td><td>I. George</td></tr>
<tr><td>10. __D.,P.__ Germany</td><td>J. Immaculate Conception</td></tr>
<tr><td>11. __Q.__ Greece</td><td>K. James</td></tr>
<tr><td>12. __R.__ India</td><td>L. Joan of Arc</td></tr>
<tr><td>13. __U.__ Ireland</td><td>M. Joseph</td></tr>
<tr><td>14. __F.,G.__ Italy</td><td>N. Mary, Help of Christians</td></tr>
<tr><td>15. __V.__ Japan</td><td>O. Mary, Mother of the Church</td></tr>
<tr><td>16. __M.,O.__ Korea</td><td>P. Michael</td></tr>
<tr><td>17. __S.__ Mexico</td><td>Q. Nicholas of Myra</td></tr>
<tr><td>18. __X.__ Philippines</td><td>R. Our Lady of the Assumption</td></tr>
<tr><td>19. __E.,Y.__ Poland</td><td>S. Our Lady Guadalupe</td></tr>
<tr><td>20. __B.,J.__ Portugal</td><td>T. Our Lady of Peace</td></tr>
<tr><td>21. __A.,Q.__ Russia</td><td>U. Patrick</td></tr>
<tr><td>22. __A.__ Scotland</td><td>V. Peter Baptist</td></tr>
<tr><td>23. __R.__ South Africa</td><td>W. Peter Claver</td></tr>
<tr><td>24. __K.__ Spain</td><td>X. Sacred Heart of Mary</td></tr>
<tr><td>25. __J.__ Tanzania</td><td>Y. Stanislaus</td></tr>
<tr><td>26. __J.__ United States</td><td>Z. Teresa of Avila</td></tr>
</table>

Your Parish Patron Saint
[Answers will vary.]

Almost every parish is named after a saint or after a feast of Christ. Find out about the saint your parish is named after or about a saint who is associated with the feast of Christ your parish is named after. **Answer the following questions:**

1. What saint is your parish named after? Or what saint is associated with the feast of Christ for which your parish is named? _____

2. When did this saint live? _____

3. Where did this saint live? _____

4. What did this saint do? Why is he or she honored as a saint? _____
_____
_____

5. When is this saint's feast day? _____

6. How can this saint be a role-model for you? _____
_____
_____
_____

7. In the space below, draw the symbols or emblems of this saint.

[Symbols will vary.]

Advent: Waiting for the Lord
Activity 1

Times of Waiting
[Answers will vary.]

Much of life is spent in waiting. Below are some examples of waiting. For each example, think of a time in your own life when you experienced this type of waiting. Tell about your experience. Then try to remember how you felt when you waited.

1. Waiting for someone to get ready

My experience:

How I felt as I waited:

2. Waiting for the school bell to ring

My experience:

How I felt as I waited:

3. Waiting for a family vacation to begin

My experience:

How I felt as I waited:

4. Waiting in line at the grocery store

My experience:

How I felt as I waited:

5. Waiting in line at a movie theatre

My experience:

How I felt as I waited:

6. Waiting in line at a fast-food restaurant

My experience:

How I felt as I waited:

7. Waiting for the bus to come

My experience:

How I felt as I waited:

[Answers will vary.]

---

8. Waiting at the doctor's/dentist's office
My experience:

How I felt as I waited:

---

9. Waiting for your favorite TV show to come on
My experience:

How I felt as I waited:

---

10. Waiting for the rain to stop or for the weather to clear up
My experience:

How I felt as I waited:

---

11. Waiting for fresh-baked cookies to come out of the oven
My experience:

How I felt as I waited:

---

12. Another time I waited:

How I felt:

Advent Mobile
[Mobiles will vary.]

Use the following symbols of the "O Antiphons" as patterns. Then make an Advent Mobile to remind yourself that Advent is a time of waiting for the Lord.

O Wisdom

O King of Nations

O Adonai

O Rising Dawn

O Root of Jesse

O Key of David

O Emmanuel

O Come, O Come Emmanuel

TR. JOHN M. NEALE (vs. 1, 2)
TR. JANE GUSTAFSON (vs. 3-7)

2. O come, O wisdom from on high, Who order all things mightily; To us the path of knowledge show, and teach us in her ways to go.

3. O come, O come, O Adonai, Who to your tribes on Sinai's height in ancient times once gave the law, in cloud and magesty and awe.

4. O come, O root of Jesse's stem, from every foe deliver them who trust your mighty power to save, and give them vict'ry o'er the grave.

5. O come, O Key of David, come, and open wide our heavnly home. Make safe the way that leads on high, and lose the path to misery.

6. O come, O Rising Dawn from on high, and cheer us by your drawing night. Disperse the gloomy clouds of night and death's dark shadow put to flight.

7. O come, O King of Nations, bind all peoples in one heart and mind. And bid our sad divisions cease, and be for us our King of Peace.

Christmas Gifts
[Responses will vary.]

Prepare a Christmas "shopping list" for all the people you care about. After each person's name, list one nonmaterial gift (helping with the dinner dishes, babysitting for free, and such) that you could give that person. Then make up a "gift-certificate," and give the person your gift.

Person   Nonmaterial Gift

1. _____

2. _____

3. _____

4. _____

5. _____

6. _____

7. _____

8. _____

9. _____

10. _____

11. _____

12. _____

Helping the Poor
[Responses will vary.]

Find out what each of the following organizations is doing to help the poor this Christmas. Discuss your findings with your family. Then choose one or more ways to help the organization meet its goal.

Organization	Activity	What My Family Will Do
Catholic Charities		
Catholic Worker		
St. Vincent de Paul		
Salvation Army		
Other : _____		
Other : _____		

Lenten Prayers
[Prayers will vary.]

There are five basic types of prayers: praise(adoration), thanks, sorrow for sin(repentance), petition, and simple conversation(sharing). In the space below, write your own prayers—one from each basic type. Then say these prayers throughout Lent as part of your preparation for Easter.

Praise:

Thanks:

Sorrow for Sin:

Petition:

Conversation:

What Penance Means

Here are some Scripture readings from the Sundays of Lent. Read each one and then tell, in your own words, what the reading says about penance. Finally, write your own definition of *penance* in the space provided.

Genesis 2:7–9; 3:1–7

We are formed of the clay of the earth, that is, of "humble origin." We are disobedient.

Genesis 22:1–2,9–13,15–18

God rescues us and blesses our acts of obedience.

Exodus 20: 1–17

God, our Rescuer, expects our faithfulness and obedience to the commandments concerning right living.

Ephesians 5:8–14

As children of light, we are to live good lives.

Luke 15:1–3,11–32

God welcomes the repentant child home.

John 8: 1–11

None of us is sinless; none can judge another.

Based on these readings, how would you define *penance*?

[Answers will vary.]

Penance is acknowledging our sins and weakness to the loving, forgiving God, and reforming our ways, thus being reconciled to God, to other people, and within ourselves.

Easter Customs
[Answers will vary.]

Some families have special ways of celebrating Easter. Maybe they buy new clothes or cook a meal of ham or lamb. In a small group, brainstorm about different Easter customs. Describe these customs in the space below. Then select one custom and tell, in your own words, how the custom relates to Easter and the resurrection of Jesus.

Different Customs

1.

2.

3.

4.

5.

6.

7.

8.

9.

10.

Custom chosen:

How it relates to Easter and the Resurrection:

Easter Cards
[Cards will vary.]

One way to build community is to send friends notes of cheer or cards that say " I'm thinking of you." Use Easter symbols(butterflies, spring flowers, eggs) to make a card to send to one of your friends or relatives this Easter.

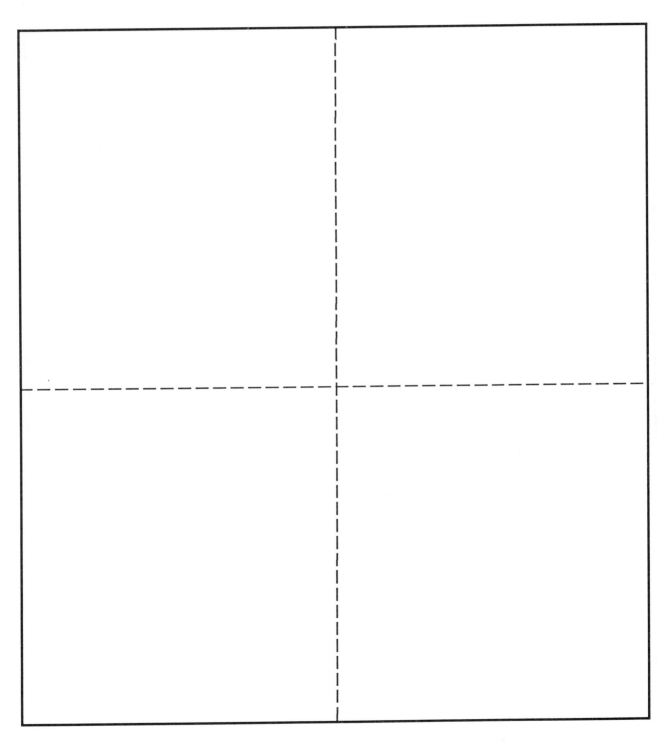

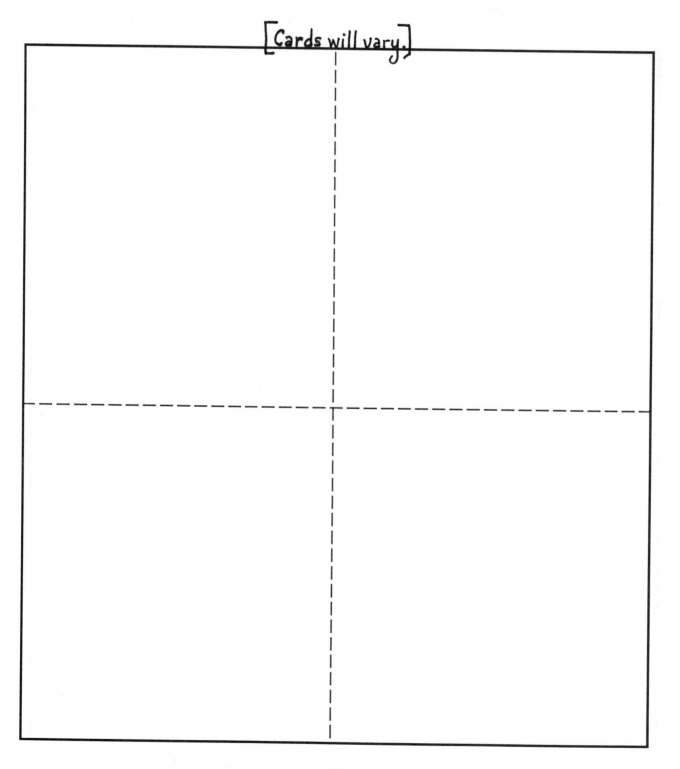

[Cards will vary.]

A Diary of Events
[Responses will vary.]

In the space below, keep a record of the ordinary things you do each day of this week. Then record the feelings you had as you did these ordinary things.

The Week of:_____

Monday
Tuesday
Wednesday
Thursday
Friday
Saturday
Sunday

Ordinary Time
Activity 2

The Cross of Jesus
[Summaries will vary.]

Read each of the following Scripture passages. Summarize each one and tell, in your own words, what it means to you.

Matthew 10:38–39
Summary:

What it means to me:

Matthew 16:24–26
Summary:

What it means to me:

Philippians 3:7–11
Summary:

What it means to me:

Matthew 11:28–30
Summary:

What it means to me:

What crosses have you had to carry so far?

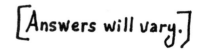
[Answers will vary.]

What are your present feelings toward these crosses?

84

A Letter of Thanks and Love
[Letters will vary.]

In the space below, write a rough draft of a letter to someone who has shown you love this past year. Recall some of the times you spent together or things you did together. Thank the person. Then copy the letter on good stationary and see that the person gets the letter.

Date:_____

Dear_____,

_____

_____

_____

_____

_____

_____

_____

_____

_____

_____

_____

_____

_____

_____

love,

_____

Joyful Times

In the first box, make a list of all the joyful times you can remember from this past year. Select one of these times and then, in the second box, write a poem about it.

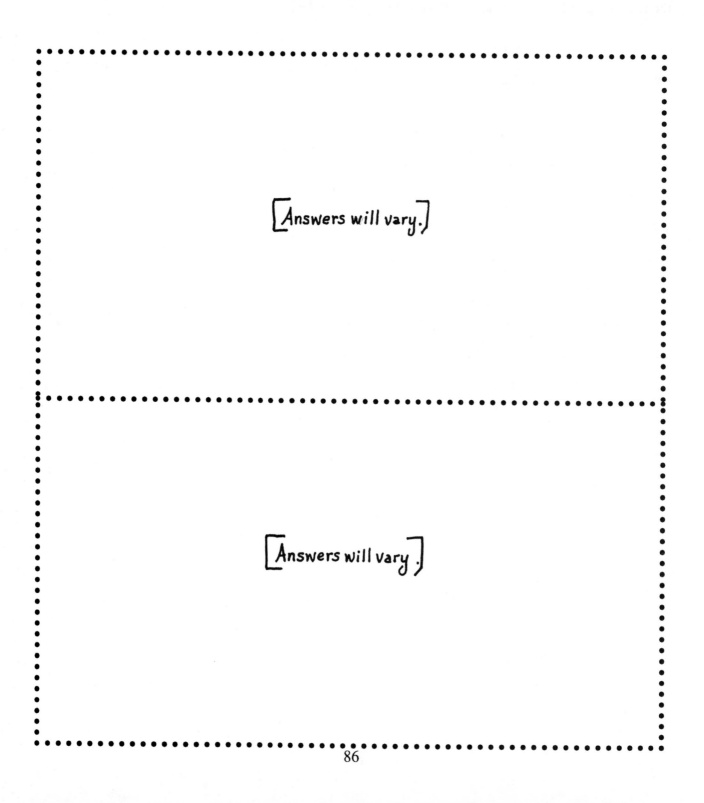

[Answers will vary.]

[Answers will vary.]

Sad Times

In the first box, make a list of all the sad times you can remember from this past year. Select one of these times. Then, in the second box, write a paragraph telling what persons, events, or beliefs helped you get through this sad time.

[Answers will vary.]

[Answers will vary.]

Glorious Times

In the first box, make a list of your achievements and moments of glory throughout this past year. Just making it through seventh grade is a big accomplishment! Then, in the second box, design a ribbon or certificate to award yourself for something you accomplished that no one else may have noticed.

[Answers will vary.]

[Answers will vary.]